SCHOLASTIC discover more™

Birds

By Penelope Arlon and
Tory Gordon-Harris

Contents

Literacy Consultant: Barbara Russ, 21st Century Community Learning Center Director for Winooski (Vermont) School District

Natural History Consultant: Kim Dennis-Bryan, PhD

Library of Congress Cataloging-in-Publication Data Available

ISBN 978-0-545-66773-9

10 9 8 7 6 5 4 3 2 1   14 15 16 17 18

Printed in Malaysia   108
First edition, July 2014

What is a bird?

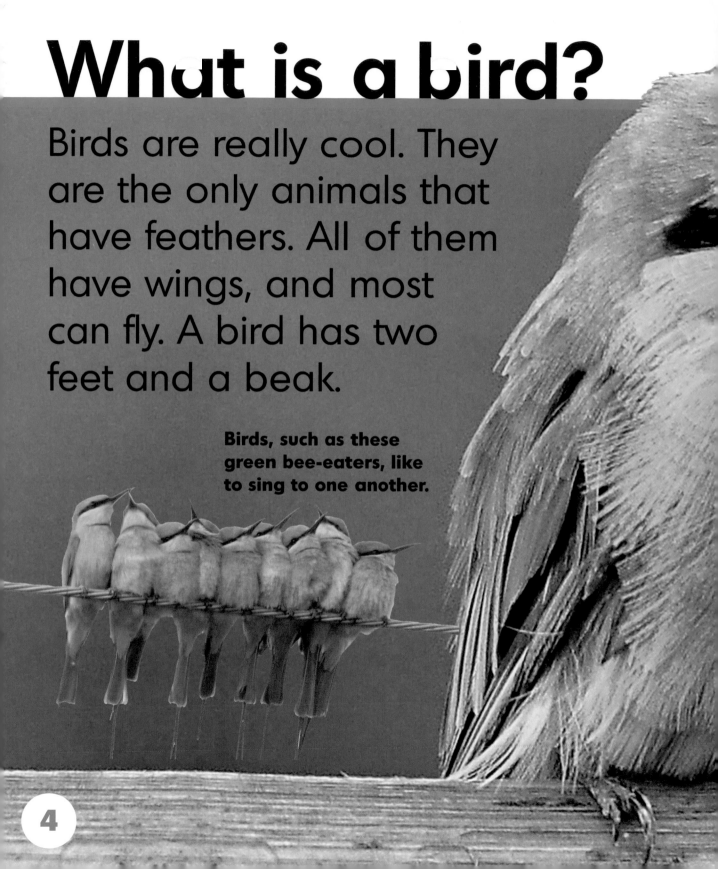

Birds are really cool. They are the only animals that have feathers. All of them have wings, and most can fly. A bird has two feet and a beak.

Birds, such as these green bee-eaters, like to sing to one another.

All birds lay eggs. Most look after them until the eggs hatch into chicks.

Dinosaur bird

Did you know that birds are related to dinosaurs? Some dinosaurs had feathers, just like birds do.

Cool colors

There are over 10,000 colorful kinds of bird!

long-tailed finch

mountain bluebird

Anna's hummingbird

American goldfinch

scarlet tanager

great spotted woodpecker

great horned owl

secretary bird

mallard (duck)

keel-billed toucan

blue tit

purple finch

chaffinch

Gouldian finch

rufous hummingbird

red-and-green macaw

Indian peafowl

pheasant

common kingfisher

flamingo

wyandotte (chicken)

mandarin duck

rainbow lorikeet

Feathers

Look for feathers on the ground. Can you tell what each type of feather is used for?

Feathers can be oily to keep birds dry.

long wing feather

fluffy body feather

stiff tail feather

Feathers have different jobs.

Birds use long wing feathers to fly. Stiff tail feathers help them change direction in flight.

Small, soft body feathers keep a bird warm and snug. They trap warm air against the bird's body.

Some birds use their feathers to show off! The male peacock fans out his amazing tail feathers.

The color of a bird's feathers can help it hide against a background. This is called camouflage.

Flying high!

Have you ever wondered where birds are flying? They fly to travel, find food, or escape danger.

Swifts fly long distances every year. This is called migration. Curved wings help them glide. They can even sleep in the air!

A hummingbird flaps its tiny wings so fast that it can hover in the air while it sips nectar from flowers.

A penguin can't fly. It uses its wings as paddles and "flies" through water instead.

A bird flaps its wings up and down. Air is pushed down. This lifts the bird into the air. It's flying!

Birds that fly have hollow bones. These make them light, which makes flying easier. A bird's whole skeleton may be lighter than its feathers!

pigeon skeleton

hollow beak

pigeon

We can't fly!

Some birds aren't able to fly. But they are pretty good at getting around in other ways!

greater rhea

The kiwi, of New Zealand, doesn't need to fly. It has no natural enemies on land.

Penguins are the best bird swimmers. They also walk and slide on ice.

The cassowary can run and swim. Some can also jump twice their height!

The ostrich is the biggest bird in the world. It is too big to fly, but it can run as fast as a racehorse!

flightless cormorant

emu

steamer duck

takahe

Brilliant beaks

A bird's beak is perfectly shaped to eat its favorite foods! Some beaks catch fish. Some beaks crack nuts.

A long beak helps the toucan save energy. It can reach fruit in trees without moving!

Beaks come in all sorts of shapes and sizes! They are used for grooming and for fighting, as well as for eating.

buzzard: tears flesh

Atlantic puffin: grips fish

Australian pelican: traps fish

flamingo: sifts water

blue-and-yellow macaw: cracks nuts

kiwi: senses bugs

mallard (duck): dabbles in water

brambling: cracks seeds

Super senses

Birds have pretty powerful senses. They can often see and hear far better than we can!

A barn owl has one ear slightly above the other to pinpoint the smallest sounds. The owl swoops silently toward its prey.

white-faced owl

A kingfisher can see clearly underwater so that it can catch fish.

A king penguin mom can hear her chick among thousands!

A vulture can sniff out dead animals to eat.

Storks have sensitive beaks. They can feel fish brushing past.

Using its sharp eyesight and hearing, the barn owl catches a rat and eats it whole!

Fantastic feet

Wings are cool. But birds have neat feet, too!

A chicken has toes with strong claws. It scratches for food.

A heron has long, thin toes that help it balance as it wades in soft mud.

A finch has three forward-facing toes and one facing back, for perching.

An emu has three thick toes for running and kicking.

A duck has webbed feet. Skin stretched between its toes helps it paddle.

An eagle has long, sharp claws called talons, to grab prey.

This blue-footed booby has blue webbed feet!

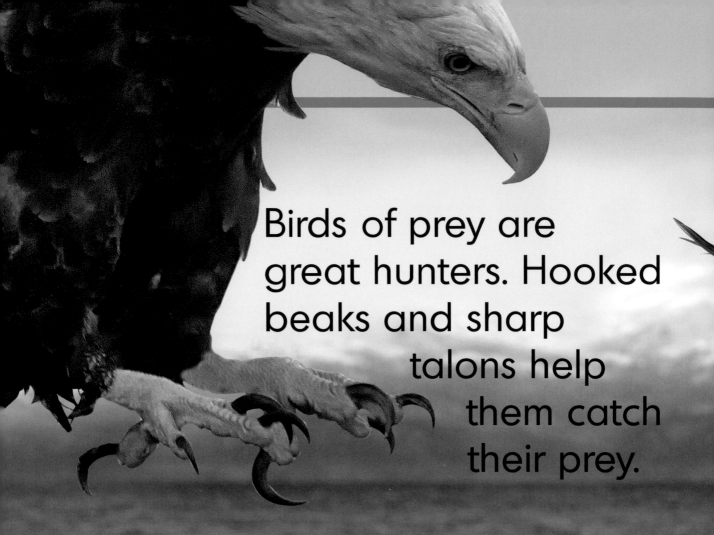

Birds of prey are great hunters. Hooked beaks and sharp talons help them catch their prey.

There are about 200 types of owl. Their special feathers let them swoop silently down on prey.

An osprey dives down to catch fish from 60 feet (18 m) in the air. One toe can turn to help grip fish.

Birds of prey

red kite

hawk

eagle owl

falcon

buzzard

This bald eagle has 7.5-foot-long (2 m) wings that allow it to fly fast or glide smoothly.

A secretary bird hunts small animals—even snakes! It stamps on a snake with its large feet.

Vultures eat large dead animals. They have bald necks, to avoid getting bloody while they eat.

Making nests

Nests keep eggs and chicks safe. Some birds build amazing nests!

Birds build nests out of twigs and soft things like animal fur.

22

Different nests

Some birds build round nests in trees. Both parents often help build them.

Owls may find holes in trees to nest in. The chicks hide inside.

A weaverbird's nest hangs from a branch. The door is at the bottom!

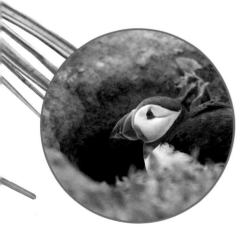

Puffins dig burrows. They line them with leaves, grass, and seaweed.

Some birds don't make nests. They lay spotted eggs on the ground.

Storks can build nests high up on chimneys!

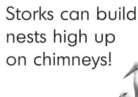

Hatching eggs

Baby birds grow inside eggs. The eggs must be kept warm and safe until they hatch.

The yolk of the egg is food for the chick until it hatches.

From egg to bird

robin quail chicken

emu

In the spring, a female blue tit builds a nest in a tree. She uses moss, fur, and feathers.

The mom lays one egg a day. She sits on the eggs to keep them warm.

Both the mom and the dad feed their chicks.

After about 19 days of feeding, the chicks are ready to leave the nest.

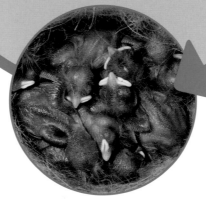

The chicks hatch after about two weeks. They are blind and bald.

25

Chicks!

Chicks are cute, but they are hard work! Most chicks need to be looked after until they grow adult feathers.

gull

Flamingos and their chicks live in big groups to keep extra safe.

26

parakeet

duckling

sparrow

owl

king penguin adult

Some chicks are born with fluffy feathers. These fall out, and adult feathers grow. This is called molting.

king penguin chick

Baby birds have to learn fast! When their wing feathers have grown, chicks in high nests jump out. They must figure out how to fly very quickly, or else . . . *bump!*

Record breakers

Weirdest beak

The sword-billed hummingbird's beak is longer than its body!

Longest feather

The tail feather of the male crested argus is nearly 6 feet (1.8 m) long.

Longest travels

The Arctic tern travels 50,000 miles (80,000 km) every year, from the Arctic to the Antarctic and back!

Heaviest flyer

The kori bustard is the weight of a five-year-old. It's the heaviest flying animal.

Most feathers

Swans have more feathers than any other bird. Some swans have up to 25,000 feathers!

Fastest bird

The peregrine falcon is the fastest animal on Earth. It dives from the sky at 200 mph (320 kph).

Smallest bird

The bee hummingbird is tiny. It's so small, it's almost as small as a bumblebee.

Longest beak

The Australian pelican's beak can be up to 18.5 inches (47 cm) long.

Best talker

The African gray parrot can copy hundreds of words. It can also whistle and make alarm and tool sounds!

Stinkiest bird

The hoatzin, of the Amazon Rainforest, is pretty stinky. It smells like cow poop!

Loudest bird

The three-wattled bellbird makes a loud *bonk* sound. It can be heard 0.5 miles (0.8 km) away!

African gray parrot

Glossary

bald
Without feathers or hair.

beak
A bird's hard, pointed jaw.

bird of prey
A bird that kills and eats animals and other birds.

burrow
The underground home of a bird or other animal.

camouflage
Natural coloring that helps birds or other animals blend in with their surroundings.

claw
A hard, sharp nail on a bird's foot.

dabble
To splash in water.

feather
One of the soft, warm parts that cover a bird's body.

glide
To move smoothly through the air, without flapping.

groom
To clean yourself. A bird grooms its feathers with its beak.

hatch
To be born by breaking out of an egg.

hollow
Having empty space inside.

hover
To hang in one place in the air.